# THAT
# FAMILY CIRCUS
# FEELING

## by Bil Keane

**Andrews and McMeel, Inc.**
A Universal Press Syndicate Company

Kansas City ● New York

ISBN: 0-8362-1125-1
Library of Congress Catalog Card Number: 81-72010

First Printing, March 1982
Second Printing, August 1982
Third Printing, November 1982
Fourth Printing, April 1983

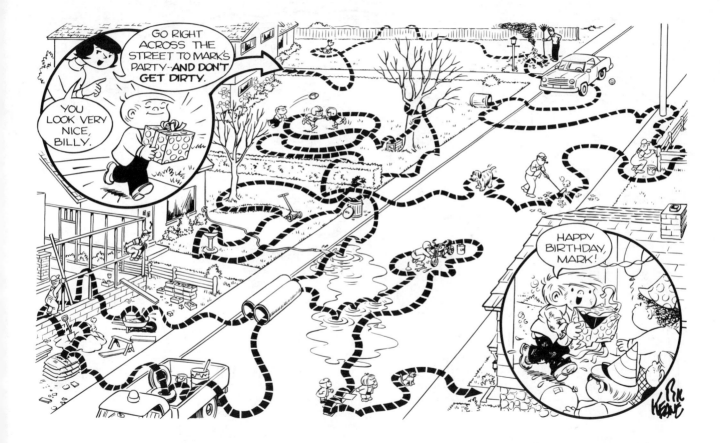

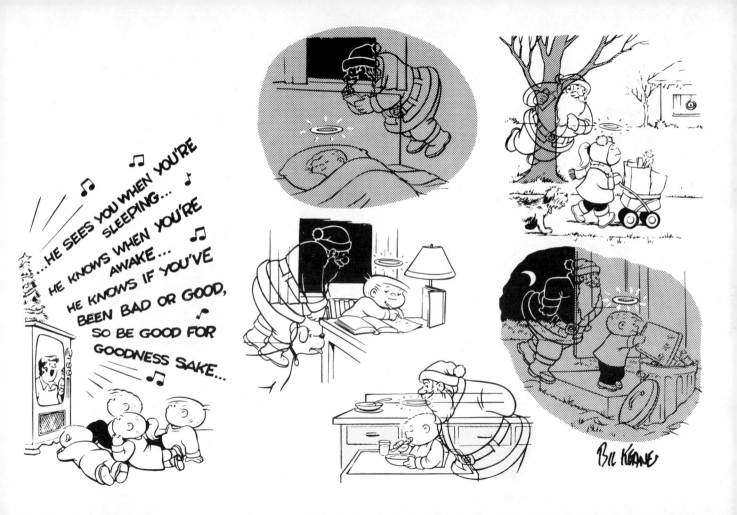